CAREER
CONTROL

Everybody has a light, a purpose, a dream inside of themselves. Some dreams are close to the surface; others are buried inside, pushed down from years of self-doubt, insecurity, fear or from life just happening.

So there you remain, stuck in hesitation and unhappiness, so far away from what is possible.

Don't you think it's time?

"Mr. Graceffa's writing is meaningful, approachable and leads you to the practical steps required to truly own your career. His, "take action" approach inspired me to conduct a gap analysis between my current skills and my next career steps."

– DonnaRenee Cook
MBA, PMP, CSM

"Jamie provides the guidance and tools for individual analysis and choice. He enables every single reader to think about things in a different way, to see potential for specific development and to become grateful and happy for their career journey."

– Claudia G. Reusch
Managing Partner,
Restracon

"Career Control provides a fascinating, contemporary, and inspiring perspective on career management. It offers an absolutely spot-on framework with insightful and heartfelt content as well as exercises from which to explore and contemplate ultra-important career impacting factors."

– Shawn Milligan
Senior Vice President,
Financial and
Banking Industry

"Brilliant! This book is a must read for anybody that has a job or wants a job. If you're just starting out or looking for your next move, Career Control will help you think through what is possible for your career."

– Rose Clervil
Clinical Social Worker
Socio-Cultural Center
for The Children of Siloe

"Career Control should be required reading for all employees. Whether you're happily employed or struggling with the need to change, Jamie's concise and insightful words take you on a methodical and logical journey with numerous opportunities to take action. Bravo!"

– Kristen Reeves
Global Client Manager

CAREER CONTROL

LOVE THE JOB YOU'RE IN OR THE ONE YOU WANT

"Jamie Graceffa turns his book into your own private career coach. Take his advice and his exercise to heart. You'll feel like he is right there talking directly to you. Great encouragement for anyone who feels stuck along the way!"

– Beverly Kaye
Founder and Co-CEO of
Career Systems International

Jamie Graceffa

    https://www.facebook.com/careercontrol
@JamieGraceffa

For information, inquires and comments, please write to: sales@bestworklife.com

To Rob,

Thank you for your endless support, love, guidance and encouragement. Life happened when I met you.

To Mom,

There aren't enough words to thank you for all that you have done for me. You are brave, strong, brilliant, and kind. You are my hero.

PREFACE

E verybody has a light, a purpose, a dream inside of themselves. Some dreams are close to the surface; others are buried inside, pushed down from years of self-doubt, insecurity, fear or from life just happening.

When we are working outside of our purpose, we long for something else. We are restless, distracted, wondering why we are here and what it is we are supposed to be doing.

When we find our purpose, we are settled, comfortable, content, fulfilled, centered, self-assured and confident in the work that we do, as it fits like a glove. It feels natural and intuitive. When you step into your purpose, you will know it.

When I started to pay attention to my career and took steps to move it forward, things started to click for me. I would see the world through a different lens, a more open and centered lens. I felt like the universe was in sync with where I was heading and it was my job to understand what the universe was showing me, find the lessons to be learned, grow from them, and take action.

I have lived the principles in this book and have never been happier in my career, which is still a journey. I am still doing the work necessary to go even further, as there is more I want to do, and more I want to say.

Whether your dreams are at the surface or buried deep, if you do the work, you will discover what is possible for you, move closer to the work you are meant to do and eventually step directly into the light of what will be your purpose.

Let's talk about the word "purpose" for a moment. I know for many people this word seems trendy, grandiose, unattainable or too big to grasp. It can be quite stressful; all these people running around putting pressure on themselves to find their purpose. Some feel that finding their purpose means helping thousands of people, or finding a cure for the common cold. If this is how you are feeling, let me take that burden off your shoulders right now.

I choose the word "purpose" to describe my own career journey. The word purpose resonated with me. This book is about helping you move closer to the work you love to do, to use your gifts for the work that is meaningful to you, and to find harmony in your job. You can easily exchange the word "purpose" for fulfillment, contentment, happiness, impassioned, gratification, bliss or satisfaction. Simply choose a word that resonates with you.

CONTENTS

INTRODUCTION

I'm going to give you a little history of who I am, a bit about my childhood dreams, and my career journey. I want to show you my journey before you embark on your own and to get you thinking about your childhood dreams.

When I was a little boy, I wanted to be two things: famous or a teacher. Oh, and bionic, but that's another story. Let's start with my desire for fame. I am not sure when it started, but very early on, I would say age eight or so, I knew fame was what I wanted. In my young mind, I had two choices: I could be a singer, or I could be on TV, like in Three's Company or Happy Days. I clearly remember debating the two choices with myself. If I were a singer, nobody would see me; they wouldn't know who I was. This was before the dawn of MTV, and all we had was the radio. What was the point of being a singer if nobody would know who I was? By the way, it never entered my mind whether I could sing or not. To me, being a singer was a viable choice, and I couldn't be bothered with such details as singing ability.

I pondered my second choice, TV. Back then, in the 1970's and 1980's, there was a TV show called Battle of the Network Stars. This entailed the big three networks, CBS, NBC and ABC, sending their television stars to compete in various athletic and sporting events. I was not a very athletic kid; I loathed gym class and generally was not very secure with myself. I thought if I were on TV; I would have to compete in the Battle of the Network Stars. I didn't think I had a choice. I thought it would be mandatory like gym class, and that scared me, so becoming a teacher was looking better and better.

I loved classrooms, teachers, chalk and chalkboards, lessons plans, pens, pencils, notebooks, and attendance sheets. The odd thing was I wasn't crazy about actually attending school. I much preferred being the teacher than the student.

My Aunt Nancy was a teacher, and to me, she was a star! Every time I saw her I would barrage her with questions: Do you have chalk? Do you write on the board? Did you put any kids in the corner? What are you teaching? She was wonderful and answered all my questions.

As I grew up and experienced school, K-12, the idea of becoming a teacher didn't appeal to me any longer. Some teachers were great, others not so much. I didn't like junior high school as I was picked on a lot. High school was better, but not enough to make me want to run out and earn a teaching degree.

On the night of my 16th birthday, I filled out and submitted an application to work at McDonald's. I worked as a crew person, got promoted to trainer and from there was promoted to a shift manager. There was a woman, Nancy, who used to visit the restaurant every so often. She would ask us questions about our jobs, what we liked, what we didn't like and asked for recommendations on where improvements could be made. She seemed to really care about our wellbeing, and people responded and trusted her. I thought her job was very interesting. I asked someone who she was, and they replied, "She's from personnel." I remember thinking, that job seems fun, I want to do what she does. I worked at McDonald's for just over nine years and had the absolute best experience. It gave me a great foundation for what I do today. I managed people much older than I was and learned early the value of treating everybody with dignity and respect. I would hold what we called "wrap sessions" where I would talk to a small group of employees about what makes them happy at work and where could we make improvements. I would take my findings to the store manager where he would decide what changes we would make. I interviewed people, created store activities, such as bingo night and family night, to increase business, and I trained people on how to do their job. Little did I know that planks of the bridge were being laid down, that these very skills would be key to my career.

The opportunities at McDonald's were presented to me at such a young age, and I did end up doing exactly what Nancy from personnel did. It wasn't until later, when I looked back in time at the signs that were shown to me and the people that were put into my path, did I connect the dots. I realized what my gifts were and understood that I had them all the time and that using my gifts would lead me closer to my purpose and that ultimately I would step into my purpose.

My parents never went to college. They were both 19 when they married, but they did just fine, and we lived a comfortable middle-class life. My dad owned his own business as a barber, and my mother stayed at home with my brother, sister and me. She later went off to work in the social services field where she worked her way up to the director level. She had an incredible amount of responsibility and was very well respected.

I tell you this because at home, college really wasn't discussed too often. I do remember my mother asking me if I wanted to go to college, but I just wasn't sure if I did.

I learned from my friends that if I did decide that I wanted to go to college, I would need to take the SAT exam, which I did. I scored okay but didn't have the grades to get into a four-year college. So I took some time off and kept working at McDonald's. I felt lost. Becoming a teacher wasn't in the cards for me, and I thought more and more about wanting to become famous.

I figured music would be my ticket to fame, so I bought a book about how the music industry worked and how to get a record deal. I recorded a demo tape of original songs and mailed it out to record companies. I waited for a response, which never came, and that is all that I did. I was too insecure, unsure of myself and afraid to leave home and head to either New York or Los Angeles, the places where one is more likely to start a music career.

I just wanted it to happen, to be discovered, without putting in the work. This is never a good approach and of course, my music career never happened. I started to think about college again and felt that it was time to shake things up.

People told me if I didn't go straight to college right after graduation; I would never go. Not true. I went to a community college, did very well and then earned my bachelor's degree in sociology with a minor in psychology from Framingham State College. I later continued on and earned a master's degree in management from Cambridge College.

While earning my bachelor's degree, I left McDonald's and started work at Pizzeria Uno, which was part of my shake up. I waited tables, bussed tables, tended bar, became a trainer and also helped with recruiting summer help. Once again, I was using the skills that would lead me to what I am doing today. At that time, I simply thought about it as work, fun work, which I enjoyed doing. I didn't know I could make a living doing this type of work.

I worked with two types of people at Uno's: those who chose a career in the restaurant industry and those who viewed the job as a pit stop until they got a job in their chosen field.

One day my co-worker, Michelle, told me she got a job. "In what?" I asked. She replied, "In human resources." I only recall two of the duties she said she would be performing: conducting new employee orientations and training. I had experienced work orientations before and did some work in training, and I liked what both duties would entail. I remember thinking to myself, 'That's what I'll do, too!'. This started my journey into the corporate world.

I had zero experience working in corporate America, and someone suggested I call a temp agency to get my foot in the door with a company and gain some experience. So I called a local agency and in two weeks' time; I had a job answering the phones. That job lasted three weeks. I told anybody that would listen to me that I wanted a job in HR. I still worked part time at Uno's and would often tell business people that came in for lunch that being a server was temporary, and I was looking for a job in HR. I was on a mission, and nothing was going to stop me! Some of my customers actually tried to help and the company I answered phones for later called me to see if I was interested in a job in HR. By that time, I had already found a job. It pays to network; it pays to let people know what you want to do and what you're interested in.

I got another temp job, but this one was more complex than answering phones. It involved using a stamp machine, Excel and PowerPoint. I had no idea what I was doing, and I was ultimately fired from the job. The employer told the temp agency that I was a very nice person, but not qualified for the job. The temp agency told me they just got a call for an HR job, a temporary to a permanent position at Belmont Springs Water Company. The agency told Belmont Springs that they had someone (me!) that had no experience, but had a great personality and was dying to get into HR. Belmont Springs' reply, "We'll take him!"

I began working at Belmont Springs in April of 1997.

I started as an HR assistant and about six months later; I was promoted to HR Representative. About a year into the job, my manager, Berni, left the company, and I was promoted to HR manager. I learned so much at Belmont Springs. I got a crash course as a generalist; I conducted orientations, touched on benefits, recruiting, employee relations, team effectiveness and training.

There was a woman, Linda, who would come up from the corporate headquarters located in Marietta, Georgia, to roll out various training events, and I would assist her. I drew upon my experience from McDonald's and Pizzeria Uno's. I loved doing this work and was good at it. Linda later certified me as a facilitator and that certification, for me, has been worth its weight in gold as I use this skill set almost every single work day.

I started to notice a theme and a trend emerge with regard to my work, which was training and development. This started formally at McDonald's, but if I go back even further, it started when I was a kid playing school. I saw what the type of work Linda did and said to myself, 'I want to do what she does!' Yet again, a person was put in my path to show me what was possible, and like the woman from personnel who worked at McDonald's I ended up doing what Linda did, too!

After spending three years at Belmont Springs, I felt that I had outgrown my role, and I wanted more.

In August of 2000, I started my job as an HR manager with Getronics, an IT solutions company based in Billerica, MA. You may be thinking, 'why did you get another job as an HR manager and not as a training manager?' That is an excellent question, and the only answer I have is that I still wasn't truly tuned into what I really wanted to do, and I am not sure I thought I was qualified for that type of job.

I liked my job at Getronics and loved the people. I got more into the training aspect of my job. In particular, I volunteered to co-facilitate a three-day workshop on managing people performance at our other US locations and in China and Malaysia. It was an incredible experience, but it was a small part of my role, and I started to get antsy. I wasn't feeling fulfilled. My job felt like, well, just a job. Most of the work I was doing was unexciting to me, and I longed for something else.

During the time, reality shows were popping up all over and that fame bug started biting me all over again. Getting on a reality show to me seemed like a perfect idea. I really did not need a talent; I just needed a personality, which I had. I thought, I will just get on a reality show, and then the world will see me and the doors of opportunity will open wide, and I would get everything I ever wanted.

In January of 2006, while still working at Getronics, I was cast in a FOX reality show, titled Unan1mous. Nope, that's not a typo; the number one replaced the "i" as there would only be one winner. Clever, right? The premise of the show was this: there were nine contestants living in an underground bunker, there was a 1.5 million dollar prize at stake, and all you had to do was convince everybody else living in the bunker that you deserved the prize money (you can't vote for yourself). I made it to the end, but ultimately did not win the prize money, which, after the show's twists and turns, was roughly 382K. Our show had a great time slot, just after the American Idol results show, resulting in between 12-14 million viewers per week.

I didn't win the prize money, but I got something much bigger than that. I was famous! My lifelong dream was met at the age of 38. Sure, it was reality fame, but I didn't care. To me fame was fame, and I felt very lucky to have it, no matter how short-lived it was. People knew who I was; they asked for autographs and photos. I was actually mobbed a few times and absolutely loved it. As quickly as reality fame comes, it goes, but I didn't care. I had it and was grateful for it.

The show ran from March to May, eight episodes. I remember the CFO at Getronics asking me what I wanted to do when I grew up. I wasn't insulted; I really liked this man and we worked well together. He asked the right question. He knew my head wasn't in the game and wanted to know my plan. I told him I wanted to do something else and left the company in August of 2006.

The reality community told me I would have to move to Los Angeles for me to really stretch out the 15 minutes of fame I had achieved. That didn't work for me. My life was in New England. There were several significant influencers that kept me from moving, namely my family, my then partner (now my husband), the fact I didn't have the money and the main reason, simple fear. I was afraid to go. I was afraid to leave home.

Needless to say, my influencers and fear made it difficult, to say the least, for me to really go for anything after the show ended. I felt lost, depressed, and disappointed. My stint on television did not prove to be the catalyst to my new career in the entertainment field. The doors did not open, and soon after the show ended, people no longer knew who I was, and I decided to go back to the work I knew, HR.

I started work at Philips Healthcare in March of 2007, and I really didn't like it all. I loved what I did, and I loved the people I supported from an HR standpoint, but I didn't like most of the people on my team, my HR team. One of my key work values is to like my team and my boss, and this was missing in my first 18 months with the company.

During that time, I worked with a woman, Connie, whose full-time job was in learning and organizational development, which she did very well. Yet again I found myself thinking, 'I want to do the type of work she does.' And yet again, eventually I did.

I wanted so desperately to either get out of the company or the department I was currently working in, so I began interviewing for new jobs internally as well as externally.

An opportunity presented itself, which involved taking a lateral move, and I took it. I started to like my job more. I liked my boss and the team I was working on. I started to do more of the work I really enjoyed: facilitating, teaching, and working with teams.

My boss knew I liked this type of work and would offer me up to do it whenever and wherever it was needed.

In 2010, I learned that my HR team would be merging with another HR team due to a reorganization. I happened to love the team we would be joining as I knew them well and liked them very much.

The learning and organizational development director Bev, on my new team, needed help, and I raised my hand. I said to her that I would do whatever work she needed me to do, and I soon discovered there was no shortage of work. I did everything she asked me to, in addition to my day job, but I didn't mind the work load. I was honing my skills and setting my reputation as an effective facilitator and trainer.

I eventually ended up reporting to her, and about nine months later she left the company. I went to her boss, Lynn, the VP HR, and asked her to give me a chance and promote me as the head learning and organizational development. She gave me a chance.

This was a dream job for me. Sure it was at a higher level and pay, but I was doing the work I loved doing, that I have been doing in some way, shape or form since I was 16 years old. I was no longer famous, and my dream of being a teacher had long since faded, but I realized that I am a teacher. Sure, not in the traditional sense I dreamt about as a kid, but I am teaching people, the only difference is that my students are adults in the corporate world and not children and my classroom is not in a school, but rather a training room inside a company. I thought, 'maybe if I paid attention to signs earlier, I would have been doing this type of work sooner.' I quickly dismissed that thought as I knew this was my journey; it was meant to be the way it came.

As an added bonus, my new boss, Lynn, is simply one of the most incredible people I have ever met, or worked for. She is kind, smart, calming, fearless and nurtures talent when she sees it. She saw a light inside of me, a passion for the work I was doing and gave me an opportunity that changed my life and the direction of my career.

In 2011, one of our initiatives was to roll out a career development program as our employee engagement survey continuously suggested that career development was an area we as a company, could improve on. So we partnered with Career Systems International, a Beverly Kaye Company and created and launched the program we titled Career Enhancement, which was extremely well received. We would teach employees how to manage their career and worked with people managers on how to help support their employees' career aspirations. A key component to the program was that each participant would meet with a career coach for one-on-one coaching, and I was one of the coaches.

Meeting Beverly Kaye was a defining moment in my life and career. She is a pioneer in the field of career development and wrote several books including Love 'em or Lose 'em and Help Them Grow or Watch Them Go.

I learned from her how each person needs to take control of their own career and do the work that makes them happy. I also learned that career planning doesn't always mean a promotion or leaving the job you're in.

Beverly ignited a fire inside of me. The work of helping others manage their career completely and totally resonated with me. This, in large part, was due to my own career journey, moving from being unhappy in my job to being deliriously happy in my current role. I wanted to share what I knew, what I learned as a career coach and what I experienced firsthand so that people could feel the same way I do about their career.

Beverly still inspires me to this day. I refer to her as my career fairy godmother. She, along with Lynn and others have led me to my purpose, to help others live their best work life, and I couldn't be more grateful.

Due to the success of the Career Enhancement program, I have been invited to speak at events and share what I know and what I have learned about managing my own career and helping people manage and develop their own careers.

Since the start of the program, I have talked to hundreds of people about their career and have learned so much from their individual stories, struggles and successes. One of my favorite questions to ask is, "How do you feel on a Sunday night, with the start of the work week just hours away?" Their answers are very telling...

1

THE SUNDAY NIGHT BLUES

Have you ever had the Sunday night blues? You know, "I can't believe I have to go back to that place tomorrow!" That place, of course, being work, or prison as I have often heard it referred to, including from myself!

The Sunday night blues, or in some cases it's the Monday night blues or Wednesday night blues (whatever fits your schedule), hits too many of us. A recent CBS news survey suggests that 55% of Americans are dissatisfied with their jobs! We feel stuck, we are miserable and so are the people around us, as they have to listen to us grouse about everything that isn't right with our work world.

I know how you feel. I've been there. I've had the Sunday night blues many, many times. So often, in fact,

I wished for an antibiotic to help cure me of this "illness" I caught and couldn't shake. I was envious of the rare individual who loved their job, who couldn't believe they were getting paid to do their work. I wanted to slap them silly, but not before I extracted their secret formula of being happy in their job right out of them!

I had the blues for any number of reasons, take your pick: I work with jerks, my team doesn't respect me, I'm not comfortable with my boss, my boss is clueless, I don't like the work, I'm under-utilized, I'm not passionate about my work, I'm not paid enough, people don't like me, I'm passed over for promotions, and my reputation, whether warranted or not, is in need of repair.

So, there's my list. Do some of my gripes ring true for you? Perhaps some of you are thinking, 'Jamie, grow up, nobody chained you to the desk of those companies, just do something about it!' Perhaps others are thinking, 'Poor Jamie, I can't believe you had to put up with that, shame on them!' If you fall into either of those two camps, then I've got you thinking. You are already drawing on your own approach, beliefs, thoughts, experiences and attitude about career, and that is exactly the frame of mind I want you to be in when you read this book.

In fact, let's pause for a moment. Write below one or two words you would use that describe your career or your attitude toward your career. There is no need to go any deeper than this. Just reading this book will uncover the reasons behind your words.

_____

This book is designed to have you think through and evaluate each aspect that pertains to one's career. There are parts of this book that may be uncomfortable, asking you to look inside yourself and consider what you haven't done to enhance your career, who you've blamed for your unhappiness and what excuses you've used for what isn't working with your career. I invite you to stay with me, get honest and be courageous as you start your journey. What I have learned from my own career journey is that there is no antibiotic, no quick fix, and it's not something someone else can do for you. You must take full ownership and take control of your career. Too many people are so willing to put their careers in the hands of others. What we do for a living is a major life choice, right up there with whom we choose to marry or partner with or where we live. We work for 50 plus years. We devote a minimum of 40 hours per week at work. It seems we spend more time with our co-workers than our families. You owe it to yourself to take control over your career and start living your best work life, and I feel privileged to be your coach.

There are several areas that impact a career, and we will cover them all in this book.

- Influencers
- Skills and interests
- Career values
- Career aspirations
- Reputation at work
- Brand
- Network
- Relationship with manager
- Childhood dreams

After reading this book, you may find yourself focusing on just one or two of these areas or all of them. It's important first to evaluate them and then decide what action you will take to enhance your career and live your best work life.

2

WHO OWNS YOUR CAREER?

I hope the answer doesn't surprise you, but YOU DO! You own your career. Earlier in this book I talked about taking responsibility and owning your career. This is critical to any change you want to make.

Is owning the choices and decisions you make in your life a no-brainer for you, something you've been doing all along? Or is this a new way of thinking that may be difficult because you are unsure of yourself or uncomfortable because you don't want to hurt people's feelings?

Think for a moment about your very first job. How did that job come to be? Did your parents tell you should work at the local grocery store so they wouldn't have to drive you to work or did you have some say in where you wanted to be employed? My first job was McDonald's. Why McDonald's? I didn't have to wear a tie; I knew a few people who already worked there, I liked the food, I was familiar with McDonald's, it paid well ($3.75 per hour) and it was close to home. There were many other places I could have worked in the area as this particular McDonald's was part of a plaza. I made the decision to work there based on my 16-year-old idea of career values and interest. I didn't know these career terms at the time; I made the choice intuitively. I knew what I wanted, and I made the decision.

Take a few minutes and reflect on the questions below. It will help give you an indication as to how easy or difficult it may be for you to take control of your career.

- Who chose the college or school you attended?
- Who chose the trade or field you worked in?
- Who chose your college major?
- Who chose the place you worked?
- Who chose what sports you played?
- Who chose what clubs you joined?
- Who chose your prom date?
- Who chose the first car you bought?
- Who chose where you first lived on your own?
- Who chose where you last vacationed?

So, who chose? Who was in the driver's seat and made these decisions? Don't get me wrong, it's very important to seek feedback, and ask advice about a decision you are considering, but when you ultimately made the decision, was it something you really wanted? Did you feel good about the decision you made? Who did you make the decision for, yourself or someone else?

Take a moment and write down some of the things you learned about yourself when it comes to making your own choices.

INSIGHTS ABOUT MYSELF:

Now that you have this insight think about your career. Who is making the decisions and choices for you there? What do you need to do to start gaining control over your career?

_____

_____

_____

_____

_____

POTENTIAL ACTIONS TO TAKE:

_____

_____

_____

_____

You have one life to live, and you should spend your time doing work that excites you and that you enjoy. I can't stress the importance of owning the career decisions you make. You can't put the power of career in someone else's hands, and why would you? Nobody knows you better than you.

3

READY! SET!
OH, I DON'T KNOW...

We just talked about ownership, and hopefully you are right there with me on its importance, but if you're not ready to take action, the concept of ownership won't help you take control and enhance your career.

I have encountered several people who simply complained to everybody about everything that wasn't right with their work world. They were unwilling to take responsibility and do something about it. They blamed other people and situations, and rarely looked inward to consider how they contributed to their own career dissatisfaction. I have also witnessed the amazing transformations of people who said to me, "You're right! I am going to stop whining, take control and get myself to a better place."

If you are unsure, uncomfortable or even scared

about making a change or a move, reflect a bit on the questions below. After reading through the questions, write down what insights and thoughts come to mind. You may get to the core of your hesitance, which can help get you unstuck. What are you complaining about?

- Who have you blamed for what's not right with your career?
- How did you contribute to your career dissatisfaction?
- What are you afraid of?
- If there is fear, what can you do to overcome it?
- Is somebody holding you back, trying to hold you down?
- What is keeping you from using your gifts?
- What have you done to try to improve the situation?
- What is possible for you?

INSIGHTS ABOUT MYSELF:

_____

_____

_____

_____

_____

Now that you have given it some thought, what might you do to improve your situation? Who can you talk to? What is one tiny step you can take?

POTENTIAL ACTIONS TO TAKE:

_____

_____

_____

_____

_____

I used to feel frustrated with the individuals I coached that had every excuse in the book as to why they couldn't do anything to enhance their career, but what I learned is that they were afraid and unsure of what to do. So there they remained, stuck in doubt and unhappiness, so far away from what is possible.

While taking actions to enhance your career, you may encounter people that will want to hold you back and keep you small. This is their insecurity speaking, and you should not listen. They are afraid you just might make it, which would further illuminate their own career dissatisfaction and lost dreams.

Stand strong in your confidence and self-respect.

Gently, yet firmly correct people who treat you in a manner that is anything less than acceptable. When you learn this, you are unstoppable; they can't hurt you. You will be less afraid to live with purpose, and this can set you free.

4

INFLUENCERS

When you evaluate your career, it's critical that you consider the influencers that could potentially impact how you enhance your career. It's not just the influencers at your company or the industry you work in, or would like to work in, but it's also about what's happening in your personal life.

Reflect a bit on the work and home influencers listed below. How do they impact your career?

Work Influencers

- Is your company reducing its workforce?
- Are there changes in senior management?
- Is your company growing?
- Is your company closing some of its work locations?
- Is your company moving work to overseas?

- Is your industry stable?
- How does technology impact what you want to do?
- Are your skills current?

Home influencers

- Did you just have a baby?
- Did your child just go off to college?
- Did you just get married?
- Did you just get unmarried?
- Are you mobile?
- Do you care for a family member?
- Do you have financial constraints?

Which one of these influencers plays a key role in your career? What creates limitations? What fosters possibilities? You don't want to start down the path and then later learn that where you were heading isn't a viable option.

HOW MAY INFLUENCERS IMPACT YOUR CAREER ACTION PLAN?

_____

_____

_____

5

SKILLS AND INTERESTS

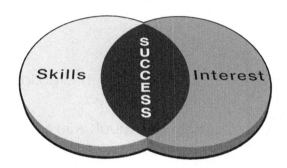

A common theme I hear a lot from the people I talk with about their career is that they are not doing the type of work they delight in doing.

The Skills and Interest exercise below will help you identify which skills you enjoy and motivate you, which skills burn you out, which skills you would like to develop further and which skills you should avoid all together.

*****

Below are 52 general skills. Each skill has a title and a description below it. Carefully read through each skill and place a number value from 1-4 in the place provided next to the title of the skill. Think about what best describes your competence and interest level with each skill.

1 = High competence/high interest

2 = High competence/low interest

3 = Low competence/high interest

4 = Low competence/low interest

*****

COACH ___
Help others think through a problem, situation or task.

MENTOR ___
Advise, educate or help individuals with less experience.

STRATEGIC THINKING ___
Identify, plan and develop long-term goals and the means to achieve them.

COMPOSE ___
Create or write music, stories, articles, materials, reports or presentations.

INTERVIEW ___
Thoroughly question for information.

BRAINSTORM ___
Generate ideas, thoughts, solutions and plans.

FORECAST ___
Accurately predict an outcome, event or trend.

KEEP RECORDS ___
Accurately maintain records and archive information. Document facts or processes.

DESIGN ___
Create, enhance or plan products, programs or processes.

COMPUTER SAVVY ___
Understand and have knowledge of computers, software and programs.

EDUCATE/TRAIN ___
Inform, provide and explain information, lessons or instructions.

ENVISION ___
Imagine possibilities for the future.

ANALYZE ___
Logically examine each aspect of a situation or problem.

BUDGET ___
Estimate finances for planned expenditures.

RESEARCH ___
Study and obtain detailed information and data.

EDIT/REVISE ___
Change, alter or amend documents, materials, writings and presentations.

GRAPH/MEASURE ___
Measure the outcome of a situation, event, product, program or process.

CALCULATE ___
Work with numbers. Think through and solve numerical equations.

INNOVATE ___
Enhance, design, or create new applications to something established.

SALES ___
Monetarily incentivized to sell and promote goods and services.

PUBLIC SPEAKING ___
Demonstrate, present or give information to a public audience.

CRITICAL THINKING ___
Use logic and reason to identify strengths, opportunities, approaches and solutions.

MANAGE PEOPLE ___
Plan, direct, supervise, develop and coordinate work activities.

TIME MANAGEMENT ___
Prioritize tasks and timetables to achieve maximum productivity. Meet deadlines efficiently.

PROBLEM SOLVING ___
Analyze information and evaluate results to arrive at the best solution.

CUSTOMER FOCUS ___
Identify customer needs, solve problems and continually provide the highest quality service and product.

PROJECT MANAGEMENT ___
Determine project urgency, create detailed action plans, and allocate and use resources properly.

TECHNICAL ABILITIES ___
Understand and apply technology, hardware, software, equipment and processes.

QUALITY IMPROVEMENT ___
Maintain high standards. Test and correct errors. Ensure accuracy in documentation and data.

LEADERSHIP ___
Facilitate decision-making and encourage action. Set vision and strategy and inspire others to follow.

NEGOTIATE ___
Explore positions and alternatives to reach outcomes that gain acceptance of all parties.

MOTIVATE OTHERS ___
Ignite excitement. Inspire others to take ownership and pride in work and performance.

PRESENT ___
Effectively communicate to groups of people and respond to questions.

MAKE DECISIONS ___
Consider costs, benefits, assumptions and facts. Choose the most appropriate course of action.

COLLABORATE ___
Share ideas, concepts and thoughts with others to reach maximum results.

ADMINISTRATIVE ACTIVITIES ___
Maintain information, process paperwork and schedule meetings, travel and events.

ORGANIZE ___
Arrange and plan projects, programs and events in an orderly and structured manner.

CONCEIVE ___
Mentally form and develop ideas, concepts and possibilities.

CREATE ___
Make or produce something new.

CATEGORIZE ___
Place someone, something or data into a particular class or group.

CONSTRUCT ___
Form, build or fix something by assembling or combining parts.

ILLUSTRATE ___
Sketch, photograph, draw or paint.

CHANGE MANAGEMENT ___
Effectively apply the tools, processes, skills and principles for managing organizational transition.

ADJUST TO CHANGE ___
Easily adapt and thrive in different conditions and environments.

PERFORM ___
Dance, sing, act, stand-up comedy, play music or speak for an audience.

WORK WITH EMOTIONS ___
Listen, sympathize, express concern, encourage and earn trust. Help with emotional wellbeing.

MONITOR ___
Observe, watch and take notice.

IMPLEMENT ___
Execute a decision, plan, process, agreement or event.

MEDIATE ___
Intervene between parties in dispute to facilitate agreements or reconciliations.

DELEGATE ___
Give control, responsibility and authority to someone.

PARTNER/LIAISON ___
Contact with and between customers, vendors, individuals and groups.

COMMUNICATE ___
Prepare and distribute written information on various subjects.

*****

Now that you've evaluated each skill, determine which 7-10 skills are most important to you in each of the four categories provided below. Then think through what potential actions you may want to take when finalizing your career action plan.

1 = HIGH COMPETENCE/HIGH INTEREST

These are the skills that motivate you that you truly enjoy using. If you are looking for a job, make sure these are the skills you put on your resume. Look for jobs where these skills are required. If you are in a job, talk with your manager about bringing more of these skills into your work. What projects or assignments can you take on that involve using these skills? If you are performing very little to none of these skills in your current job, is this the job you want be in? If not, which jobs interest you?

List your top 7-10 skills from this category:

_____   _____

_____   _____

_____   _____

_____   _____

_____   _____

POTENTIAL ACTIONS TO TAKE:

_____

_____

_____

_____

_____

2 = HIGH COMPETENCE/LOW INTEREST

These are your burn out skills. You can perform them well, but you are tired of using them. If you are looking for a job, remove them from your resume, otherwise you will get calls for jobs that necessitate using these skills. If you are currently working, speak with your manager about minimizing these skills and add other duties that encompass the skills you love to use. Perhaps there is a co-worker that enjoys performing some of the skills that burn you out. Can your manager horse-trade projects and work within your team in a way that plays to individual strengths and interests? Where can they reduce burnout and increase motivation? Your manager may find that where one employee dreads project plans, another employee will salivate just thinking of deadlines and RACI charts. You can also get creative and work with your colleagues to propose a plan to your manager that redistributes the work based on the interests of the team. You will never know unless you ask!

List your top 7- 10 skills from this category:

_____   _____

_____   _____

_____   _____

_____   _____

_____   _____

POTENTIAL ACTIONS TO TAKE:

_____

_____

_____

_____

---

3 = LOW COMPETENCE/HIGH INTEREST

These skills are your development opportunities. How much development you need depends on how competent you are performing the skill. If you have a basic understanding of the skill, you may want to expand your knowledge and build on what you already know. You can find a coach or a mentor who is exceptional at the skill you want to develop. Connect with them and learn how they perfected that skill and put it to use. The best way to develop a skill is to use it. Try taking on a project or assignment where you will have to use that skill. Be careful not to flex the skill you are trying to develop on a time sensitive or highly visible project. Start small and build your way up. If you are completely unskilled, take a class, read a book, search YouTube, Wiki pages or any other type of social media and learn the fundamental knowledge of the skill. Then follow the suggestions above.

List your top 7-10 skills from this category:

_____   _____

_____   _____

_____   _____

_____   _____

_____   _____

POTENTIAL ACTIONS TO TAKE:

_____

_____

_____

_____

_____

4 = LOW COMPETENCE/LOW INTEREST

These skills are of no interest to you. They are unimportant and do not motivate you. You should avoid using them. If the majority of your work consists of performing any of these skills regularly in your job, you want to consider if this job is the right one for you.

List your top 7-10 skills from this category:

_____   _____

_____   _____

_____   _____

_____   _____

_____   _____

POTENTIAL ACTIONS TO TAKE:

_____

_____

_____

_____

_____

6

CAREER VALUES

Career satisfaction isn't only tied to your salary, benefits package, and the type of work you do. Our career values are things in life that you value in relation to work and have a direct correlation to career satisfaction. Career values give purpose and meaning to your job.

Rank the following career values according to the importance you place on each of them. Rank no more than 20 career values, with 1 being the highest importance and 20 the lowest.

Recognition	____	Achievement	____
Autonomy	____	Wealth	____
Health	____	Integrity	____
Work/Life balance	____	Loyalty	____

Control	____	Competitiveness	____
Collaboration	____	Creativity	____
Power/Status	____	Physical Challenge	____
Respect		Growth/ Advancement	____
Security	____	Efficiency	____
Spirituality	____	Responsibility	____
Fun	____	Learning/ Education	____
Harmony	____	Acceptance	____
Self-actualization	____	Intellectual challenge	____
Influence of others	____	Location	____
Service of others	____	Authority	____
Leadership of others	____	Freedom	____
Compatibility with team/boss	____		

Add your own values that may not be listed:

_____

_____

List your top 7-10 career values:

_____ _____

_____ _____

_____ _____

_____ _____

_____ _____

Which career values are being met? Which are askew? Talk to your manager about your career values and develop ways to improve where needed.

If you are looking for a job, seek opportunities that are in alignment with your career values. For example, if you value work/life balance, and your potential dream job will have you traveling 50% of the time, you may want to think twice about considering that job. Career values aren't always obvious in job postings so if you get to the interview stage make sure you ask questions about the career values that are important to you.

POTENTIAL ACTIONS TO TAKE:

_____

_____

_____

_____

_____

7

CAREER ASPIRATIONS

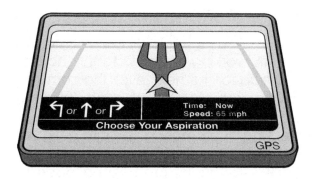

Some of you are in jobs that you really like and don't want to leave, but something is missing. It's become a bit stale, a bit mundane. Enhancing your career doesn't mean you have to give up a job you enjoy, run out and get a college degree or change fields... or does it? It is all up to you and what you want to achieve.

Below is a list of possible career aspirations. Place a check mark next to the career option or options (limit to two) that work best for you. You want to think of the reality of your situation. How probable is it for you to jump two levels from your current job? You may need to gain more experience and development before that is possible.

Enhance the job you're currently in ___

You want to stay in the job you're in as many people do. You like your job, but what can you do to love it?

Review Chapter 6: Skills and Interests, and Chapter 7: Career Values, and determine what actions you will take to enhance your job. Work with your manager to incorporate more of the work you like to do and the values that you hold important.

Advancement/Promotion ___

You are seeking a higher-level job or promotion. If you're currently working, it's important to note that even if you're qualified for the next level, the company won't create a job or promote you into a job just because you're qualified for it. There has to be a business need to warrant creating or promoting you into a higher position. Be patient, talk to your manager, let them know what your plan is. If there are no promotional opportunities in sight, consider another career option.

Lateral move. Similar job level and similar pay ___

You may consider this option to gain exposure, develop a skill that you don't currently possess or better align with your career values. Some people choose this as their first option in order to move to the advancement/ promotion option.

Reduced role, less responsibility ___

You may have a life event, influencer or situation where a lesser role is a better fit for you. You also may consider this option to gain exposure, develop a skill that you don't currently possess, or better align your career values. Some people choose this as their first option in order to move to the advancement/promotion option.

Unsure, need to explore what's out there ___

It may not be clear to you what you want to do. Interview people that do work you find interesting. Ask them what a typical day looks like, what they like most and least. What are their challenges, obstacles and motivators, and what inspires them about their job? Take on an assignment in your areas of interest. Take advantage of a job rotation program, should your company offer it, or observe meetings and events where you can, as you gain immense insight by observation. It's imperative to be well-informed before taking a new job, or you may regret your move.

Relocate from current work location ___

You may have a life event or influencer where you need to move and want to stay with the company, or the job you really want is in another location and you are willing to move for it.

Exit the company ___

If you did everything in your power to enhance your career and the company has not responded in kind, it may be time to pursue other opportunities. Be sure that your new job entails the work that interest and motivates you and that your career values are met. The last thing you want to do is leave the company and realize you made a big mistake.

POTENTIAL ACTIONS TO TAKE:

_____

_____

_____

_____

_____

8

REPUTATION

A reputation can be made in an instant and, if not good, take much longer to repair. Something as simple as an email exchange can ignite a reaction, followed by a judgment call, and there you have it, a reputation is born! Right or wrong (and we've all heard this before) perception is reality. A person's reputation can make or break their career.

Many times a person seeking an internal move, who is well-qualified technically, may not be selected due to their poor reputation. The typical answer back to these individuals as to why they didn't get the job is that it wasn't a skill match. A bit of trickery you say? Maybe, but theoretically, it's true. Being able to interact well with others at work is an absolutely critical skill to possess.

Think for a moment about yourself. What would a group of co-workers sitting around the table having lunch say about you, should your name come up? Does it match what you would want them to say? If you don't know, maybe you should find out. And how does one find out? The answer is simple: feedback.

Feedback is a gift, as they say, and similar to gift giving, you may not always like what you receive. If your reputation needs work, ignoring it is not going to help you, nor will it make the perceptions about you less real. That said, people are not always willing to volunteer feedback, and even if asked directly for it, you may get a response lost in a coat of sugar or, even worse, be told that no issues exist.

Why is this? People want to be nice or not hurt feelings? Maybe, but in some cases, it's those same individuals that will grouse to everybody, but you on where you fall short. Not so nice after all.

If your reputation is in need of repair, ask your manager about participating in a 360-degree feedback assessment. This process involves select individuals and groups of people that have high visibility and insight into a person that is seeking feedback. All responses other than those from the managers are anonymous. The person seeking feedback also has an opportunity to rate themselves and see how aligned they are or aren't with other assessments. Once you have this information, you can decide what action you will take to repair your reputation.

Kindness Counts

A key element of a positive reputation is kindness,

which is often underestimated in the business world. Every action has an intention, a designed purpose. What are your intentions, your true intentions as opposed to your disguised intentions, when interacting with people at work? A true intention is the reason why you are taking the action. A disguised intention is masking the reason why you are taking the action.

For example, you are in a meeting, and colleague is presenting an update on a key project. You start firing question after question, challenging their data, and you do so in a very direct, unsupportive and rude manner. Another attendee of the same meeting pulls you aside when the meeting ends and asks you why you were so hard on the presenter. You reply that you care about the presenter and want the project to be successful and that you were only trying to help.

If this is the case, it is your true intention. Your delivery is poor, and you need to do the work to improve it otherwise your true intention will not equal the impact on the presenter or anybody else you want to provide feedback to.

If this is not the case and you meant to embarrass the presenter or throw them off because they did the same thing to you at a previous meeting, then this is your true intention, and what you told the fellow meeting attendee was your disguised intention.

If your intentions are designed to hurt, embarrass or hold somebody down, what are you trying to soothe, heal, numb or repair inside of yourself? If you pause for just a moment and think about your true intention, you may decide to tweak the action or do away with it all together. This is another great way to start to repair your reputation.

If your intentions are to help, support or lift somebody up, then good for you! My guess is that your reputation is in good order, and you model behavior that fosters collaboration, success and teamwork.

Having said all of this, you can't please everybody and you shouldn't try to do so. There are some people who, no matter how hard you try, will not give you a chance or change their mind about you. If that's the case, and the person doesn't play a significant role in what you do on a regular basis, then let it go. Maybe it's their reputation that needs work. Focus your time and energy on people that matter, who are willing and open to resetting your relationship with them. If you are looking to repair an aspect of your reputation, say composure for example, a good starting point could look like this: "John, I know I have a tendency to overreact to certain situations and lose my temper. I want you to know I am aware of it and how it negatively impacts our team, and I am working on it. I am learning to slow down and process the situation before I react and not take an opposing opinion as a personal attack on me." If you are going to take a step similar to the one just outlined, you have to walk the talk, otherwise you're in danger of further damaging your reputation.

Don't over-think your reputation or focus so much on how you come across to others. This might cause you to withhold opinions or thoughts that could lead to a better solution. Collaboration is good; healthy conflict is good, if done in a productive professional manner. Avoid personal attacks and don't get stuck in your own position. Rather, seek to understand another point of view, ask questions, be curious, keep your ego in check and LISTEN! The ability to work through a complex situation can strengthen one's reputation.

Don't be afraid to ask for feedback. If you do, be ready for it and open to it. Don't react too strongly or get defensive. Seek to understand and ask for examples, say, "thank you" and then decide what you want to do with it. Hopefully, the feedback is valuable and makes sense to you.

What this all boils down to is an awareness of how you come across to others, and the importance of sustained, positive interaction and collaboration. Model this behavior and others may follow. We're all human, and we will undoubtedly have an off day here and there. When it happens, circle back, course correct and learn from it. Your reputation is worth it.

POTENTIAL ACTIONS TO TAKE:

_____

_____

_____

_____

_____

9

BRAND

The previous chapter was all about reputation, and you may be thinking, 'Why do we need a section on brand? Aren't they one in the same?' It's true; many people view a person's brand and reputation as the same thing or very similar, but I see them as distinct.

I view brand as the "what." What you do for work, your key duties, skills and capabilities. In other words, what makes you unique.

I view reputation as the "how." Simply put, how you treat people. How you connect with others, do business, collaborate, build and maintain relationships.

For example, you may be known for being the best hairdresser in town. You give fantastic, consistent cuts; your work is flawless. Everybody you touch leaves the salon looking like a million bucks. This is your brand.

If you are consistently running late with your appointments, cancel appointments, or are unfriendly, this is your reputation and it could harm your business. Or, on the other hand, if you are always right on time, never reschedule and are upbeat and friendly, this is also your reputation, which will benefit your business.

That said, some people may not care about your reputation. They want the best there is and are willing to put up with a tarnished reputation to get what they want, but imagine the possibilities if your brand and reputation were spot on.

Think about your brand for a moment. What is it? Do you have one? Do you know what it is?

If you don't know or aren't clear on your brand, now is the time to figure it out. Knowing what your brand is and how to articulate it is very important to your career. Your brand is all about you, your gifts, what separates you from everybody else, and what you want to be known for, which is key.

What you want to be known for should align nicely with the work you love to do. Look back at chapter six and see what skills are in your high competence/high interest list. This is the work you want to be known for. When you brand this, you build awareness, and people will come to you to do the type of work that motivates and excites you. The more work you do that you love, the happier you are.

There are other things to think about to help you gain clarity and create your brand. Ask yourself these questions and record the answers:

How do I make people feel? _____

_____

How will others benefit by working with me? _____

_____

How have others described me? _____

_____

How would I describe my work? _____

_____

Who is my target audience? _____

_____

What gifts do I have to offer others? _____

_____

What makes me unique? _____

_____

What makes me great? _____

_____

Now, use these answers to develop a short statement about your brand. This is often referred to as your elevator pitch. Think of it this way: if you are fortunate enough to find yourself in the elevator with somebody that has to ability to enhance your career, you better be prepared to tell your story. Elevator rides don't last long, and it's very important that you communicate quickly, precisely and clearly about who you are and what you bring to the table. You never know when opportunity will knock, and when it does, be prepared. An elevator pitch is great for networking as well, both in social media and in person. Our collective attention span seems to be shrinking. People just read the headlines and when they do, they should have a pretty good sense of who you are and what you have to offer.

When writing your elevator pitch, make sure your statement captures the work you love to do and the essence of what makes you so special.

Here's an example of an elevator pitch of someone who is seeking a job:

Hi, my name is Chris. I was working on a project I am very proud of as an HR manager for a company where the drivers were to increase our employee engagement scores by investing our employees' development. I loved working with the managers and employees on all the creative ways a person can learn and become more successful in their job. I have a passion for learning and feel great satisfaction when people feel better equipped to do their job. I would like to be in a learning and development job where I can make a difference and do the work I truly enjoy.

Here is an example of someone who is in a job they like, but would like to do more of the work they love to do.

Hi, my name is Leslie. I am currently working as an administrative assistant, and I really like my job. Recently, I had the opportunity to plan a big sales event in Las Vegas. I loved working with the hotels, booking the travel, planning the meals, entertainment, meeting space and working with all the people attending the event. I received a personal note from the VP of sales thanking me for making the event such a success. If you ever need any help planning your event, please let me know. I would welcome the opportunity to help you out.

Here's my elevator pitch:

Hi, my name is Jamie. I am passionate about my work as a career coach. I have helped many people enhance their career and start living their best work life. I do this because I've been there; I was miserable in a job I didn't like, so I did the work to change that. It's an incredible feeling to wake up every day and look forward to going to work. I want to help as many people as I can experience this. If I can ever be of service to you or someone you know, I would welcome the opportunity.

What's yours?

_____

_____

_____

_____

_____

_____

Now that you're armed with a phenomenal elevator speech, what is your current situation? What work are people coming to you for now? Is it for work that you are uninterested in or tired of doing? If this is the case, here are a few tips you can use to change that:

When you see an opportunity to do the work you love, grab it. Even if this means doing work for people you aren't responsible for or normally don't work with.

Take on an extra project on top of your day job. If you love what you do, and are good at it, it will show. People will talk, and the word will get around. It will be extra work for you, but the benefit is that you get to do the work you love. You may find yourself in demand and filling a business need, which is a great way to do less and less of the work that burns you out.

Speak up and promote the work you love to do and are great at. Toot your own horn! When you get an email about the great work you do, forward it to your boss. They may start to give you more of the work you love to do.

Whether you are looking for a job or are in a job you like, talk to people in your network, family, friends and colleagues, especially colleagues. What does a group of work colleagues usually talk about besides office gossip? Work, of course! It's the perfect opportunity to ask your colleagues if they know of anybody that has a need for the type of work you love to do. When people talk about work they are passionate about; the excitement shines through, it's written all over their faces and other people pick up on it. I remember talking to people about my passion for career coaching and more often than not I would hear, "You know, so-and-so should talk to you, would you mind if I put you in contact?" I didn't even have to ask.

Believe in the power of your brand. We are more connected and visible now than ever before. Competition is stiff. Simply knowing, clearly knowing, who you are, what gifts you have to offer and what you are meant to do will make you stand out and be heard which will lead to you living your best work life.

10

NETWORK

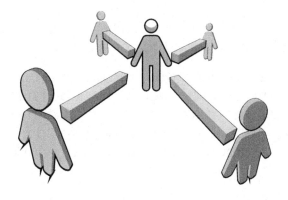

The importance and power of career networking should not be discounted. Very rarely do we find career success on our own. Be deliberate when choosing your network. It isn't about attending a networking event and collecting as many business cards as you can hold or joining 30 social media networking groups. That's too much to manage properly or gain any benefit from. It's about making connections to the people or groups that can directly help you enhance your career. Building a network of value is especially important if your manager isn't exactly tuned into your career development.

Creating and maintaining your network takes some nurturing. Don't just call on your network when you need something. Check in with your network regularly. It could be a quick call or email asking how they are or wishing them a happy holiday. You don't want to be seen as someone that is simply using people. You will wear out your welcome and people will be less likely to help you.

Consider what you can do for your network. Ask the people in network what they need and offer your help. Write a thank you note or send a small gift if somebody has really come through for you.

If you are a member of a social group, contribute the group, don't just ask for advice or information.

The people in your network can provide you with information, help you develop in your job or hone a particular skill, act as a mentor or coach, and connect you to other people. Just remember, if you don't know someone, you probably know somebody who knows somebody.

11

RELATIONSHIP WITH
MANAGER

Having a good relationship with your manager could easily fall in the career values section of this book, but because it's such an important part of your work life and directly impacts how happy you are in your job, it warrants its own chapter.

I'll go out on a limb here and declare that everybody wants to have a good relationship with their manager, but, of course, the degree of that want will vary. There are some people that tell me that they don't care who they work for so long as they get a paycheck. I do find, however, that more often than not, people very much care about having a good relationship with their manager, and if absent, it can cause a great deal of stress, frustration, anger and feelings of being trapped or helplessness. After all, it is your manager who evaluates your performance, which in most cases links to what your annual salary or merit increase will be. They may also influence other monetary incentives such as bonus pay out and stock options grants.

Your manager also plays a key role in your career development. They influence your work values, which we covered in chapter seven; they assign your work, help you with problems, challenges and obstacles, and impact your work/life balance.

You may be working for a new, inexperienced manager who doesn't know what being a good manager entails. Many times a person moves from an individual contributor to a people manager based on what they achieved when they were an individual contributor.

Being a people manager is like having two jobs. The first job is achieving the goals set forth for the year. The second job is managing direct reports, which involves a whole suite of duties, some of which are mentioned above. Many times they are put in a people manager role without any support or training. If this is the case, it usually doesn't end well for the new manager.

You may be working for a seasoned manger that's been at it for 20 years or more, and for whatever reason, they still aren't good at being a people manager. Maybe they don't care, maybe they don't know how, or maybe they do know how but don't have the time to dedicate to your development or coach you through a challenge.

No matter your situation, there are things you can do to enhance or improve the relationship you have with your manager.

The most common gripe I hear from managers with regard to their employees is how much they complain about something without offering any solutions and simply expect their manager to fix or own the problem. Do not whine to your manager no matter how valid your reasons. Whine to a trusted friend, go for a run, meditate, eat some chocolate or play with a pet.

This is not to say that you don't approach your manager with your situation. That's what they are there for, but you need to do it in a professional, solution-focused manner. Below are some guidelines for you to follow that will create a much more productive meeting.

Be clear about what the problem is, what you have done so far and what some possible solutions are. If you truly have no idea what to do next, then say so, but before you decide to tell your manager that you are without a solution, run your problem by a trusted colleague. They may see something that you don't and be able to offer some great advice.

Don't forward an email chain and expect your manager to read all the way down and back up again. Summarize the situation and clearly state what action you are seeking.

Don't throw people under the bus. If someone has dropped the ball, not returned your calls or failed to provide critical data, simply walk your manager through the situation. They will understand that the problem is with others and not you. Before you have this conversation, give the culprit the benefit of the doubt and try a few times to get what you need from them.

Be respectful of your manager's time. Don't barge into

your manager's office with a complicated problem that requires more than 5 minutes of time unless it is truly an urgent matter. If it can wait, schedule a meeting.

Know how your manager prefers to receive information. If they are more of a data driven person, give them the data and the detail. If they prefer information a high level, summarize it for them. If they are more of an email person, use email. If they prefer the phone, use the phone.

Know what their hot buttons are and avoid them. How can you find out what they are? Ask. If you have a new manager, tell them you would like to understand how they like to work and what they expect from you. Don't be afraid to ask for their thoughts on things that are important to you such as working from home or changing up your work hours. The worst that can happen is they say no. And if they do, accept it and don't label them a jerk. If your manager is not new and you are experiencing some issues, schedule a meeting, and tell them that you are committed to improving your working relationship and would like to reset. List the areas that cause the most friction and offer some ideas on how to work differently and ask for their thoughts on the matter. If there is something you need from them, don't be afraid to ask. If you need more time with your manager ask for it and explain why.

Meet commitments. If your deadlines are in jeopardy, tell your manager immediately. They should not be surprised or hear it from someone else.

Be in lockstep with your manager on what your deliverable goals, objectives and key areas of responsibility are.

Understand what's on your manager's plate, what keeps them up at night, and offer ways to help.

Be proactive. If you see a problem, address it. If you have ideas to better improve a process or situation, offer them up and take action.

Do not use social media to vent about your boss. It will come back to bite you.

Always be respectful, friendly and professional. Treat your manager and everybody else for that matter with dignity and respect. It will take you farther than you know. Your manager is a human being and is not perfect. If you have a decent, good or even great relationship with your manger, be grateful. Focus on what they do well rather than where they fall short. I think you would want the same from the people you work with, including your manager.

If you find it difficult to get along with your manager, chances are that they feel the same way, too. Bring it to their attention. Tell them what you are feeling about the relationship and ask for their view of it. Probe what you can do differently to help the situation. Be sincere and open to ideas. Share that you are committed to resetting the relationship and don't shy away from professionally asking for something you need.

I cannot guarantee that if you follow these guidelines you will have the relationship with your manager that you want, but I can tell you it will improve. It will open the lines of communication; create a more relaxed work environment and increase trust and respect on both sides.

Unfortunately, there are some managers out there that are real jerks or even bullies. They are mean for sport, difficult, unreasonable, play favorites, steal credit, embarrass you, offer no support, and are condescending. These managers are, in my opinion, insecure, suffer no consequences for their behavior, won't change, and should either be fired or placed into an individual contributor role. If you are working for a manager like this, which I truly hope you're not, talk to your human resources manager. If nothing changes, you may want to seek other opportunities and should revisit the career aspiration chapter in this book.

If you're currently employed, think now about the relationship you have with your manager. On a one to ten scale, ten being outstanding and one being dismal, where do you fall? Write your number below.

_____

What specific dynamics are in play, or missing, that determined your number?

_____

_____

_____

_____

_____

If you are seeking a job, what type of manager would you like to work for?

_____

_____

_____

_____

_____

When interviewing with a potential, future boss, ask some key, specific questions about their management style that are important to you. Their answers may indicate whether you'll be happy in the job or not.

POTENTIAL ACTIONS TO TAKE:

_____

_____

_____

_____

_____

12

CHILDHOOD DREAMS

In the introduction of this book I gave you a brief history of who I am, the steps I took in my career, and in particular, my childhood dreams.

I told you I wanted to be a teacher or famous. They were sustained dreams throughout my childhood, not fleeting thoughts. It wasn't like I wanted to be famous on Monday, a teacher on Tuesday and a chemist on Wednesday. My desires to be famous or a teacher were not flavors of the month for me; they were true dreams.

Let's break it down a bit and start with my dream of being a teacher. The headline is teacher, but what being a teacher did I love so much, what is the subtext?

- Sharing ideas and theories then having a dialog about it
- Giving information to people that they could use

- Being a catalyst to have people think about things in a different way
- Fostering ideas
- Facilitating the brilliance that collective thinking can bring
- Being front and center with a class
- And as mentioned in the introduction, I loved classrooms, chalkboards and school supplies.

With the work I do now, I feel I am a teacher. Not in the traditional K-12 classroom session I envisioned for myself when I was a kid, when my line of sight was limited. I didn't know what else was possible. I teach classes about career development in the workplace. I have students, I give them information and bingo; an exchange occurs, ideas come to light, discussions ensue and the learning spreads. This fulfills me; this feeds my soul. I still get a thrill when I walk into a training room 45 minutes before a class starts to set up. I just take it in. I don't have chalkboards, but I do have white boards and flip charts.

Now, let's talk about my other dream, fame. So what is it about fame I loved?

- Being acknowledged and recognized
- Being front-and-center, on stage in front of an audience
- Performing
- Seeing my name and photo in print
- Being interviewed
- Being on camera
- Attention

I know that these sound superficial, but they're honest, it is my truth. I also get to experience many of these things in the work I do now. When I am giving a talk to a large audience, there is production in the room, video cameras, a stage and big screens with my name on it. The event coordinators will promote my talk ahead of time, and my photo and bio are there in print.

I stand on a stage and give my talk, which in many ways is like performing. When I finish, they applaud and come up to talk to me about how much they learned or enjoyed what I had to say. I am acknowledged. But what I really love, beyond the applause and recognition is the pure happiness I feel knowing that I have reached and touched the audience in some way. That I helped them think about things differently, that they see what is possible and real for themselves, and I feel truly honored to be a part of their experience.

Now it's your turn. What were your childhood dreams?

List them in the left-hand column below. In the right-hand column, list feelings, thoughts, work, and visuals associated with your dreams.

Childhood Dreams   Feelings, thoughts, work

_____   _____

_____   _____

_____   _____

_____   _____

_____   _____

What elements can you bring into the work you do today? What is possible for you? List your potential actions below:

_____

_____

_____

_____

_____

CAREER ACTION PLAN

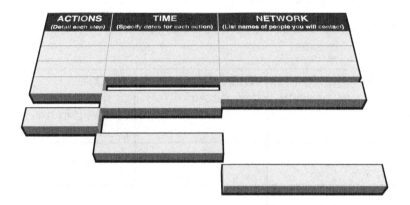

ACTIONS (Detail each step)	TIME (Specify dates for each action)	NETWORK (List names of people you will contact)

This is where where it all comes together.

Review each section of this book and decide what actions you are going to take. After evaluating each section carefully, you may conclude that you are indeed doing the work you love, but some of your career values are out of whack, and working to improve your career values will be the focus your action plan. Or you may find that building your network is what you want to focus on. You don't have to choose an action from each section. Use the areas that speak to you most, that best fit your current situation. This book was designed to meet you where you are.

It's about quality, not quantity. You can't boil the ocean. It's about creating a realistic, manageable plan and having the courage to take action on things you can achieve, which will move you closer to fulfillment, joy and to you purpose, creating a path for you to start controlling your career and living your best work life. Once you pursue your passion, you will perform more strongly than you thought possible. Happiness = success in more ways than one.

Ready? Set? GO! I know you can do it!

HOW will I get to the goal? Specify each action.	WHEN will each step occur?	WHO else is or should be involved in my plan?

Notes:

_____

_____

_____

_____

_____

_____

_____

_____

_____

_____

_____

_____

_____

_____

_____

_____

_____

_____

_____

_____

CONCLUSION

In Chapter 1, I asked you write down a few words you would use to describe your career or your attitude toward your career. What words would you use now after finishing the book? How are they different from what you wrote in chapter 2, what have you learned about yourself and what has shifted for you?

I asked the same question to groups of people just prior to a learning event on career management. Here are some of the words people used when answering the question:

Evolving, Ambivalent, Risk-Averse, Challenging, Chaotic, Stable, Passive, Exciting, Improving, Under-Utilized, Mystery, Wait and See, Repetitive, Dead End, Stuck.

A few bright spots, yes, but mostly these descriptors are disappointing, sad and alarming.

Now here's a list of words those same people used to describe their careers after they became empowered to take control and realize what is possible for them:

Enlightened, Enabling, Expand, Self-Powered, Empowered, Interesting, Energized, Talk to People, Enhance, Responsibility, Reputation, Opportunity, Take Control, Self-Promote, Self-Driven.

The difference is quite remarkable. I get so excited and happy for all of them as they being their own career journey, just as I am for you.

As I sit at Panera Bread in Waltham, MA, with my best friend of 42 years and writing partner, Doreen, adding the final words to Career Control, I am thinking about what word I would use to describe my career right now at this moment in time. My word is gratitude.

ACKNOWLEDGMENTS

Thank you, Marthe Stanek, Gale Rothwell, and Kristen Reeves for your editing genius! You gave your talents out of love, and I will not forget it.

Thank you, DonnaRenne Cook, Glenn Brewer, Shawn Milligan, Andy Palmer, Rob Nazzal, Annelyse Anderson, Matt Glotzbach, Rose Clervil, Marthe Stanek, Gale Rothwell, Kristen Reeves, Claudia Reusch, and Shamus McBride for your insightful feedback and thoughts.

Thank you, Beverly Kaye for EVERYTHING! You truly are my fairy godmother!

Thank you, Geoffrey Moore for your help, guidance and generosity.

Thank you, Richard Knowdell for sharpening my career coaching skills.

Thank you, Kerry Vincent for your guidance and encouraging me to pick up that ball and run like hell!

Thank you, Stace Rudd for your stories and counsel.

Thank you, Lynn Gauthier for leading me to this work. You truly changed my life.

Thank you, Doreen McBride, my writing partner and best friend. You were with me for every step of this book. I know your book will be a huge success!

Thank you, Daniel Von Nydeggen, for your creativity, talent and patience with me for every single rewrite, edit and tweak, we finally got there!

Lastly, thank you, Panera Bread. Career Control was almost entirely written in your establishment. I couldn't have done it without you!

Jamie Graceffa is an author, speaker and career coach. His background includes expertise in the areas of performance management, employee engagement, team transformation, and job and career development.

Notes

Notes

Notes

Made in the USA
Middletown, DE
20 August 2019